VOICES

Written by Edel Wignell
Illustrated by David Kennett

Voices
ISBN 978-0-7406-1028-8
ETA 352111

Revised American edition published in 2004 by ETA/Cuisenaire® under license from Era Publications. All rights reserved.

Text © Edel Wignell
Illustrations © David Kennett

ETA/Cuisenaire Product Development Manager: Mary Watanabe
Lead Editor: Betty Hey
Editorial Team: Kevin Anderson, Kim O'Brien, Nancy Sheldon, Elizabeth Sycamore
Educational Consultant: Geraldine Haggard, Ed.D.

ETA/Cuisenaire • Vernon Hills, IL 60061-1862
800-445-5985 • www.etacuisenaire.com

No part of this publication may be reproduced, stored in a retrieval system, or transmitted, in any form or by any means, electronic, mechanical, photocopying, recording, or otherwise, without the prior written permission of the publisher.

Printed in China.

11 12 13   10 9 8 7

VOICES

WHEN EDEL WIGNELL wrote this book, she wanted to write an animal story in a different way. So, she created Karen and Greg, two scientists studying a colony of emperor penguins — while living near them on the Antarctic ice!

"Writing *Voices* was a new experience — describing the relationship between humans and animals in the wild," says Wignell.

"I was trying to say something about the importance of communication — between animals and between humans," she adds. "Communication is and will be an important part of saving the world."

Table of Contents

Antarctic Egg	7
Scientists	10
Dance to Your Daddy	14
Penguin Chick	18
Penguin Movie	27
Harry's Growing Fast	30
Penguin Family	34
Harry's Family	39
Survival	43

Antarctic Egg

It was a freezing day in May. The female emperor penguin laid her greenish-white egg on the Antarctic ice. Quickly, she pushed it with her beak up and under a big flap of skin, which looked like an apron, below her belly.

Her mate, the male emperor penguin, was with her. They called to each other with their trumpeting voices.

Early the next day, the female penguin rolled the egg onto the male's feet, and he maneuvered it under his fatty fold. There, it was secure and warm — like a baby in a thick blanket.

The penguins trumpeted to each other again; both knew it was time for the female to go. At the same time, hundreds of other voices were raised; hundreds of penguin pairs were parting. The males would stay in the rookery to care for the eggs, while the females would seek food.

Scientists

Two scientists, Greg and Karen, stood at the edge of the rookery, watching the birds during the egg-laying.

The day before, Greg and Karen had walked among the penguins, making a film of the egg-laying and taping the penguin voices. The penguins had ignored them, for they had seen humans before. Humans had walked among them and done no harm, so the birds felt no fear.

"I wonder how the females feel about leaving their eggs?" mused Greg. He had not liked leaving his own family — his wife Jan and their girls — to come to Antarctica.

Karen guessed that Greg was thinking about his new baby son, whom he had not met. News of the birth had come by radio-telephone.

"We'll be home soon," she said. "Only four months till we leave."

"Yes, I know. I really miss the girls and wonder what our new baby is like," said Greg. "I'll send them a fax tonight."

DATE:	August 16, 2004
FAX TO:	Sue and Katy, 1-619-555-1234
FROM:	Dad, Mawson Base, Antarctica
NO. OF PAGES:	1
SUBJECT:	A fax to my darling daughters

Dear Sue and Katy,

Today, Karen and I watched the penguins laying their eggs. The female knows that her egg would freeze in seconds, so she pushes it up under a flap of skin to keep it warm and safe.

I'm wondering — is Harry a noisy baby? Well, he couldn't be as noisy as the penguins! They were deafening today — all trumpeting at once! Each one knows its mate and recognizes its mate's special voice. The females have now gone to feed and left the males with the eggs.

A big hug for Harry and both of you,
Dad

Dance to Your Daddy

The baby cried; he kicked and waved his fists. His mother lifted him up to her shoulder and patted his back while she walked around the kitchen singing.

Dance to your daddy, my little laddie,
Dance to your daddy, my little lamb.
You shall have a fishy in a little dishy,
You shall have a fishy when the boat comes in.

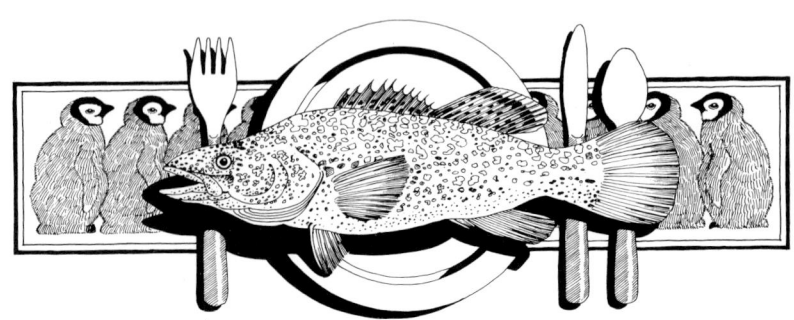

Harry burped, and his mother and two big sisters laughed.

"So that's what he thinks of fish!" said Sue.

"He's too young for fish sticks," said Katy.

"He'll make do with milk for a while yet," said Mom. "He won't eat solid food till after Daddy comes home."

"I wish Dad would hurry up."

"I wish he hadn't gone to the Antarctic. What kind of presents can you bring from there? There are no stores."

"I wish he'd gone to New York. He could've brought me a Yankees T-shirt."

"Or a Mets T-shirt!"

"Greedy kids!" said Mom, undressing Harry. "You shouldn't be thinking of presents. Just having Dad come home will be wonderful, and especially wonderful for Harry. He doesn't even know he's got a father."

She lifted Harry into the bath while Sue and Katy watched.

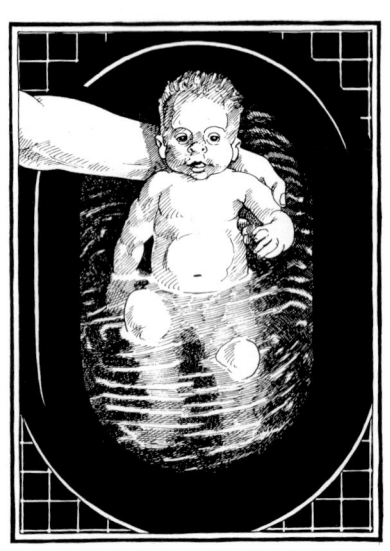

"Come on, girls. Talk to Harry."

"But he's too young to understand," said Sue.

"It doesn't matter! It's good for him to hear your voices. He knows us by our voices as well as by our faces."

"Funny face, funny voice," said Mom, making a silly face and talking in a squeaky voice.

Mom continued, "If you two talk to him every day, he'll learn to talk more easily. Tell him about his dad. While you talk, I'll take some pictures."

Katy began, "Daddy's a scientist in Antarctica …"

Penguin Chick

The female emperor penguin set off on her long, long trek with the other females from the rookery — far, far away across the ice to the open sea — miles away. A month ago, she and her mate had waddled that same distance up to the rookery, full of food, for it had been time to breed and lay eggs.

At last, the female penguin reached the sea. She immediately dove, found a squid, and ate it. Each day, she hunted for fish and squid, eating and eating, gorging herself.

As the weeks passed, she gathered a huge store of food within her body. It was like a pantry — food ready to be used later by herself and her chick.

The females swam and fished together, their voices keeping them in touch with one another. At the end of two months, it was time to return.

Heavy now, they set off — back, back, back across the icy wasteland. They pressed on, eager to return to their mates at the rookery. Perhaps their chicks had hatched, perhaps they had not. The females could not know.

Meanwhile, the male penguins had nursed the eggs along, keeping them safe from the numbing cold. When blizzards roared with cutting winds and driving snow, they drew closer together, sharing their warmth. Living on the fish and squid that they had caught in the autumn, they had grown thinner and thinner. Now, they knew it was time for the females to return.

Across the icy ridges, they saw black heads bobbing and heard voices rising up, riding on the wind. They called back, trumpeting a welcome.

The female penguin called to her mate and he called back. They called and called to each other. Through the hubbub of trumpeting, the female recognized her mate's voice and headed straight toward him. They greeted each other.

Their chick had not hatched yet, but there were many chicks nearby. The male passed the egg to the female, who quickly tucked it away.

Now, it was the male penguin's turn to make the long, long trek to the open sea. He set off and trudged along with the other males, while the females cared for the newly hatched chicks and remaining eggs.

The female penguin's chick had grown and changed inside the egg. Now, it was ready to hatch. The egg was a prison. The chick struggled — it needed room, it needed air, it wanted to be free. It kicked and heaved with its legs and wings, cracking the shell.

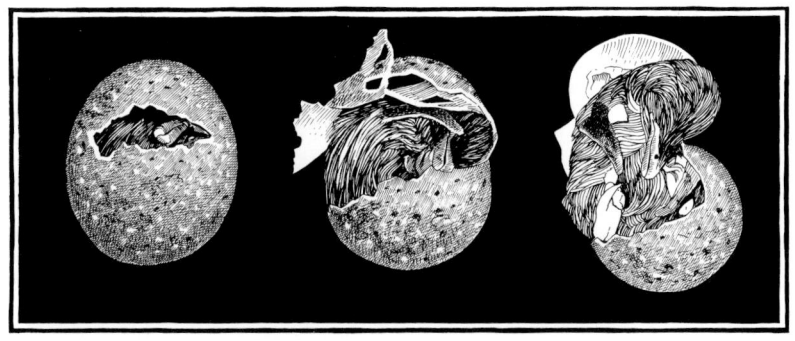

After a few moments, it kicked and heaved again, and the crack grew wider.

Out came a young male chick and opened his eyes. The wind caught him suddenly and he fell over, but his mother's beak nudged him upright.

At the same time, she welcomed him with her voice into the Antarctic world. This was the first sound he heard and he would never forget it. There were other voices, too — thousands of voices, all around. But, he heard and knew the special sound of his own mother's voice. Instinctively he knew that, by keeping close to her, he would be safe.

Penguin Movie

Karen and Greg again stood on the ice overlooking the rookery. They filmed the arrival of the females. That night, Greg sent another fax to his family.

DATE:	October 23, 2004
FAX TO:	Sue and Katy, 1-619-555-1234
FROM:	Dad, Mawson Base, Antarctica
NO. OF PAGES:	1
SUBJECT:	Another fax to my darling daughters

Dear Sue and Katy,

Your turn to get a fax. Thank you very much for your great letters and drawings. I have tacked them all up by my bed — it's a gallery!

Filming was exciting today. The female penguins returned after spending months away fishing. Each one heard her mate call and waddled right up to him. How they are able to hear each other in all that racket, I don't know!

Some of the eggs have hatched. The others will hatch in the next few days. Now, it is the males' turn to go fishing.

I can't wait to see both of you! How much have you grown? How big is Harry? I'm looking forward to seeing all the photos.

Much love to all of you,
Dad

The next day, Karen and Greg filmed the males' departure. Then, on the outskirts of the rookery, they chose a female with an egg and set up the camera there. When it was time, they made a close-up film of the downy, gray chick as it hatched — and they tape-recorded the voices of the chick and its watching mother.

Harry's Growing Fast

Meanwhile, back at Greg's home, it was Harry's bath time. He especially liked bath time on the weekends when Sue and Katy helped and talked to him.

"Daddy's coming home soon," said Sue. "You know, he's a scientist on a team from the Conservation Foundation and they're filming in the Antarctic."

"You see, Harry, although Antarctica is a frozen desert, it's got a lot of birds," added Katy.

"And huge fishing grounds all around, with seals and whales, too."

"It's got oil and minerals deep underground."

"And some companies are planning to mine them."

"What will happen to the wildlife if they do?"

"If a fishing company takes a lot of fish, there won't be enough food for the seals."

"What if they mine where there's a penguin rookery?"

"Get your camera, Sue," interrupted Mom. "Take more pictures for Daddy. Harry's growing so fast."

They took photos of Harry by himself, Harry with the girls, and Harry with his mother. He gurgled, enjoying his bath and the voices of his mother and sisters.

"Let's make a tape of Harry," said Sue. "Sing, Mom!"

Mom wrapped Harry in a towel and jiggled him on her knee as she sang "Dance to Your Daddy." Harry gurgled and laughed, and Sue recorded his voice on tape.

"We ought to tape him in the evenings,

too," said Katy, tickling Harry. "To let Daddy know what it's like when Harry shrieks and howls and won't stop."

"In another two months, Daddy'll be home," said Katy. "We ought to show him what a nuisance Harry can be."

Harry laughed some more.

Penguin Family

The emperor penguin chick grew fast, feeding on fish and squid from the female's stomach. At first, he stayed close to her body and her voice.

His whole world was the rookery, filled with chicks and female penguins.

Meanwhile, his father reached the shore and, with the other males, began to feed. In three weeks, their stomachs were full of fish and squid, and they returned.

As they crossed the stony ridges near the rookery, they trumpeted to the females and the chicks. The females answered. The males' chorus of calling grew louder, closer, and the answering chorus grew more urgent.

The chicks called with their mothers and, for the first time, heard the voices of their fathers. The male penguins heard the voices of their new chicks. They hurried on, right to the place where their own chick waited.

At last, the rookery was filled with penguin families.

But, now it was the female penguins' turn to leave and gather food, while the males cared for the chicks. The females set off once more.

Soon, the chicks became adventurous, daring to move away from their fathers and play with each other — jabbing with their beaks, slapping with their flippers, quarreling, and jostling.

They were growing up.

Harry's Family

Greg showed the movies that he and Karen had shot, and switched off the projector.

"The penguin chick will be growing up fast now," he said. "Soon he'll lose his downy coat. Underneath are waterproof feathers. He'll be playing with the other chicks."

"Sometimes several parents will go off fishing. One adult will look after all their chicks," said Karen. "Spring is coming and the ice will be breaking up, so the feeding journeys will get shorter."

"When that chick is ready to learn to fish for himself, the ocean will be at his feet."

Harry listened to the unfamiliar voices and stared at his father.

"Come here, little Harry," said Greg, picking him up and jiggling him on his knee. "I'm your dad! You'll know me soon."

"Sue, show Dad the photos you took," said Mom.

"I'll get the tapes," said Katy.

Greg looked at everyone and compared the pictures of Harry as a newborn baby with his appearance now.

"How you've grown while I've been away!" he exclaimed. "Before too long, you'll be able to talk."

Soon, Harry got to know his father and recognized his voice. He squealed with joy when he heard Dad come home from work. Harry was even eating solid food now — sometimes mashed-up fish!

Meanwhile, Greg and Karen and the conservation team were very busy producing their films about the life cycle of the emperor penguins and the fragility of their habitat. These would be shown all around the world.

Survival

As he grew, the emperor penguin chick learned to use his voice more loudly, trumpeting to communicate, trumpeting for safety and survival.

Gradually the ice melted, and by the time the great ocean was at his feet, he was ready to fish for himself.

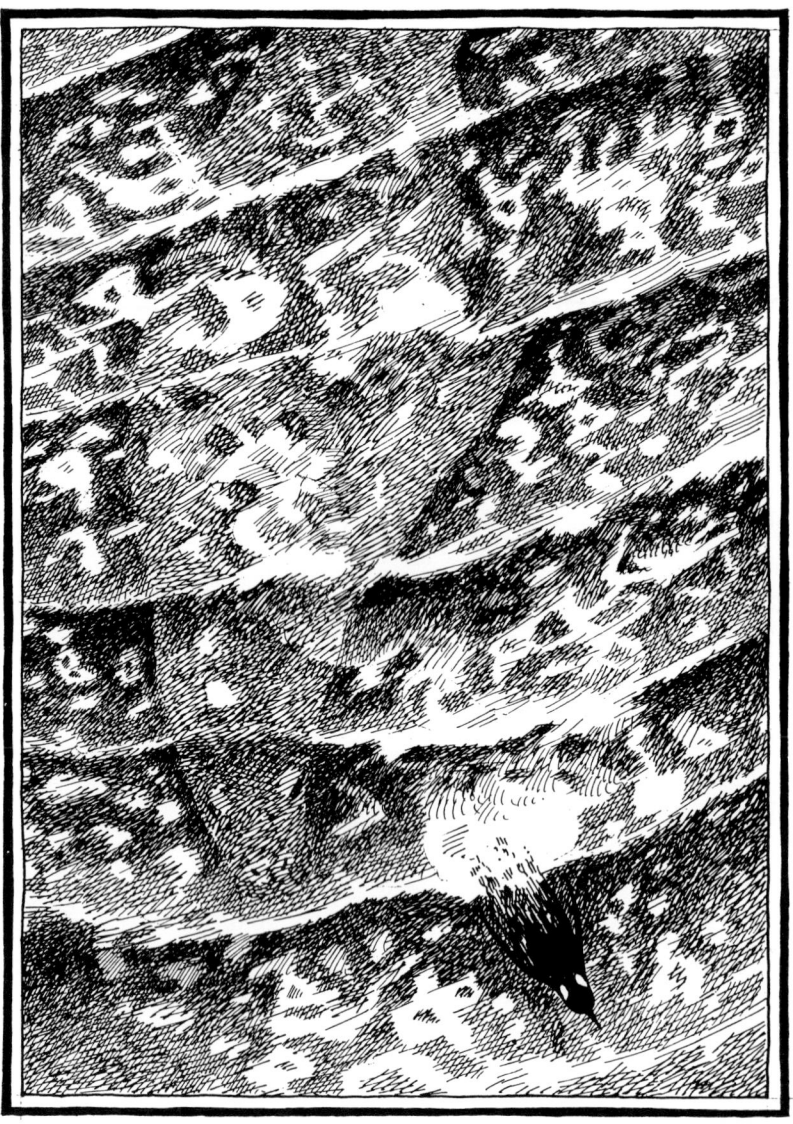

Like a torpedo, the young penguin dived for squid. A hungry leopard seal lunged at him, but the penguin dodged the lightning-quick snap of its jaws. He rocketed out of the water and soared dolphin-like through the air. Snatching a breath, he dived back and propelled himself fast toward the bank. He leaped out, landed feet first on a ledge, and trumpeted in triumph.

Safe!